BIOGRAPHY AND OTHER POEMS

BIOGRAPHY AND OTHER POEMS
DANILO KIŠ

TRANSLATED FROM THE SERBIAN
AND WITH AN AFTERWORD
BY JOHN K. COX

This is an Autumn Hill Books book
Published by Autumn Hill Books, Inc.

1138 E. Benson Court
Bloomington, Indiana 40401
USA

Book design & layout — Richard Wehrenberg
www.richardwehrenberg.com

Autumn Hill Books ISBN: 9780998740041
Library of Congress Control Number: 2018963815

AB
www.autumnhillbooks.org

ACKNOWLEDGMENTS

The translator wishes to express his thanks to Dragan Miljković and Aleksandar Štulhofer for their warm-hearted and expert tips on translating difficult passages in the poem "The Poet of the Revolution on Board the Presidential Ship."

This volume would not have been possible without the wisdom and support of Pascale Delpech and Mirjana Miočinović, and I offer them my warmest thanks. In addition, I would like to dedicate these translations to my sister, Beryl Cox Pittman, whose innate love of literature (with a refined sense of storytelling in particular), fearless curiosity, and amazing work ethic have inspired me for decades.

TABLE OF CONTENTS

BIOGRAPHY AND OTHER POEMS

Farewell, Mother

Mother, your glassy eyes trouble my spirit
and your spreading wrinkles cut my pupils...
Stone-like and blue, your lips are silent
but I hear your words, quiet and sweet.

Once more, mother, o just once more
let your warm fingers plunge into my skin
so I can feel, mother, in this icy morn
the glow of your love... And while the bell tolls

give me just one word of comfort
and shut the eye fixed on infinity,
while I sense your gaze searching me out
as across your withered face the last tear drops.

O, that tear would have so much to say:
a mother's kiss as she prepares to leave,
words of advice before she says "Farewell,"
the tender love of a mother who is no more!

(1953)

(Untitled)

I dream about you, a childhood over,
as about a girl with blue eyes.
And when your skies appear to me in a dream,
I cry with joy, the joy of your days breaking.

And I forgive you everything, as a mother does a son,
or the son his mother—however you wish—
the happiness lost, so long sought,
which you, childhood, never gave me—

forgive you the father with no resting place,
   and the mother in a grave,
and Eva—as a girl, the withered lily of my youth—
and all of it, everything taken from me
by your streams, your white streams...

And I give you pardon and open my sleeping mind
to you like the girl with the blue eyes.
And when your skies appear to me in slumber,
with a tear in my eye I shall dream of your dawns.

(1953)

Tomorrow

Every evening, weary from unfulfilled desires, but with a
quiver of hope forever in my heart, I whisper the one word:

Tomorrow!
Tomorrow someone will say to me: son;
tomorrow someone will say to me: beloved;
tomorrow she'll say to me: I... love...;
tomorrow I'll deposit all my sufferings in a grave,
in a grave without a cross, without any marker so that
no remembrance of them remains;
tomorrow...
And so on, in this way, three hundred sixty-five days a year—
Tomorrow!... Tomorrow!

(1953)

Poem About a Jewish Girl

—MOTIF FROM 1941—

Slowly the young girl, dressed for a holiday, walked along the street. On her chest she wore a six-pointed yellow star resembling a sunflower, which withers as soon as the sun sets.

After her came soldiers, one of whom carried a rope. Behind this column a curious crowd pressed forward, perhaps quieter, and treading more softly than usual.

And when the girl with the yellow star stopped beneath the gallows, she removed the hat resting upon her red hair and used it to cover the tear that plunged to the star at her breast.

The sun set, spilling the blood carried from the Jordan....

(1953)

Biography

That Eduard Kohn was a prodigious drunk.
He wore eyeglasses of glistening prisms and watched
the world through them as if through a rainbow.

1

Even as a child he had to urinate
    after the others at school, for he was circumcised.
Once he loved a baker's daughter and was a little happy.
When she learned he was circumcised, she didn't think
    she could share his bed.
From then on he loved slipping his wages to csárdás-fiddlers
    and trading kisses with Gypsies.
And then, seeking comfort, he grew fond of Deliria, and she
    wrapped him up in her sincere embrace.

2

The wind scattered his ashes through the narrow smokestack
    at the crematorium, higher and higher,
        all the way to the rainbow.

(1955)

Wedding Guests

Wedding guests are walking
out of my home

The people in black carried away
my mother

The ones in white
my sister

To my heart it all sounds the same
whether it is the bells that fire
or the cannon that toll

Wedding guests are walking
out of my house

(1955)

The Piano

1

A man
in a black tailcoat
with a knife in his chest
and teeth bared

2

A woman
in evening dress
with a blonde cartridge-belt
of a laugh

(1955)

Sunset

1

Take one ripe orange (with peel)
then two or three slices of ripe lemon
Then drive your fingers into the soft red earth,
and mix it all together

Of course this still isn't the color of sun over sea
                                        fatigued from its day
nor will the pap thicken without egg whites
So you need to tank up on red wine
and wait till it mingles with your blood.
(Listen carefully: blood sweeps through the veins
                                        like seething geysers.)

Then
when the blood boils over and the vessels swell
sever the artery on your left hand with a piece of glass
and mix the pulp like dough till it sets
and your eyes go white and your strength gives out.

2

Then you must dive in the sea
                deep down
and catch an octopus (the bigger the better)
pin it to the wall with a harpoon or nails and
slice its tentacles open lengthwise
                    with a keen razor.
Watch it dying in cold blood.
Then get a big red rose
and pluck its petals gently
                one
                    by
                          one.

(1962)

Poem About A Poem

Who will eat whom? Who overwhelm whom, and who dominate?

I arrange black and red ants on the white, icy cube and watch as they stumble, as they slide, as they spin around in circles, fall and lose heart, wander around in their new environment, as clumsily as fish on dry ground, like an albatross on land, unaccustomed to columns and formations, unaccustomed to a corporal's commands, to the whip and the hymns, dulled by brass marching songs. I make my observations, investigating them with a bit of pity, with compassion that could step onto the cutting edge of a lancet.

*

How will they orient themselves to their icy new surroundings, devoid of compassion, these tiny ants who've been driven into columns, the disobedient ones, subjugated now, the subjugated ones?

How will they get along on the icy hill where their little legs freeze and stick and their antennae have nothing to grab, nothing to touch, and nothing to do except get tangled up with each other or grope their own cold rear ends, or that of another?

*

How long will their own body heat support them, the inertia of the flow of their own blood, how long can they live on memories, on the illusory and futile memories of the warm convolutions of the uterus that hurled them pitilessly into this icy world?

For how long will they listen to the untruthful echo of their own words that have now frozen on their lips and feelers?

When will the rainbow fade from their recollections, here on this ghostly iceberg devoid of color, scent, and taste? When will their senses dull and lose the smell of fruit and of grass, the aroma of spices and citrus, the scent of females, of glebe and blood?

At some point the melodies will fade, melodies of once being in paradise that they listened to in the twists and turns of the womb, warm melodies that enticed them into this gelid inferno in a fit of frenzied enthusiasm.

*

I watch them—rendered penitent, lined up in rows, broken into pairs, cap-to-nose, stepping across the horrifying white wasteland accompanied by strains of martial music—one-two, one-two—forward, march! And, company halt! Then forward again. And even though I have seen them as domesticated, broken, and obedient and have even thought I recognized their temperament as slavish, they begin to stop, tripping and breaking ranks, out of fear, weakness, spite—or, what? —and then I lower a coiling snake onto them—to wipe them away, liberate them, fatigued, dulled by punishment, liberate them from their torments.

*

After that I watch with curiosity to see what will happen. Who is going to defeat whom, who overpower whom, who dominate in the midst of this ghastly icy hell? The serpent or the ants?

Who will eat whom?

(1957)

Still Life

WITH FISH

Two albatrosses white
in the sand

Two sapphire ships
on a reef of coral

A pair of Sirens grown hoarse
on a porcelain iceberg

WITH DOVES

Azure envelope returned
with a red stamp

Tricolor routed
in the dust

A trampled fan
of silk

WITH FLOWERS

Petrified chord
on lips of crystal

A flock of frozen birds
at daybreak

The butterflies'
graveyard

(1958)

The Lighthouse Excursion

If you get to this island, then you are, in truth, shipwrecked. Who would make such a pilgrimage out of sheer curiosity? But it is good for you to know what you are: a victim of a shipwreck. So now at least you believe in Providence (as that type of belief is designated) and you consider yourself born under a lucky star. Now you are exploring a new continent and you christen it, naturally, the Cape of Good Hope. It fits.

*

For—and why not?—no human has ever set foot on this patch of terra firma. That much, verily, is obvious. Here you are Adam, and it will not be hard to create an Eve for you (from a rib or clay or the moonlight).

And what clacks beneath your feet is surely not stone. Compared to this, stone is like cotton, while in the moonlight you cannot be sure of telling the difference between chunks of white quartz and diamonds.

*

But who erected in this wilderness a lighthouse, if I am the First Human here for real? In that case this must not be a lighthouse; it is a gigantic, insatiable firefly. Or a stray meteor squirming in the sand. Or it's like you're dreaming it all: your star is falling and you hold out your palm. In your palm—a tiny drop of dew.

*

You're already starting to think it isn't there; either the wind has blown off its petals or it has been turned into a star. And then it makes its presence known, from somewhere, like an owl. So you twist your compass in that direction, and you're off. Course set for: lighthouse.

Who wants to keep waiting for the moonlight?

*

Again you think: it's gone. You've already worn out your legs hoofing across these accursed diamonds (what was that?); branches in the undergrowth whip you bloody; and the lighthouse was a... fata morgana. Some lighthouse! You are just turning around to go back, lie down, or cry for help (maybe some evil spirit out here will hear you), when its WHOOSH-WHOOSH flashes in the gloom and you move on in that direction, with nary a thought for your feet or other trivialities.

*

One must get accustomed to the irregular rhythm of the lighthouse. Your ears have gotten too used to the fluting of an owl, the whistling of a canary, the accordion playing of a frog. But there exists a great rhythm, a counterpoint, a harmony that is not included in the textbooks of solfège. That's why you have to listen hard and forget looking for laws. You have to rely on your hearing.

And waiting for the moonlight is not necessary.

*

If you reach the lighthouse (if, as I say), climb up the tower and extract several drops of the oil that is in the lamp. Take care: leave enough for your way back. Now wait patiently for the moonlight. You have learned to think straight and you already have an ear for that grand and wondrous rhythm.

*

Look at the beauty, Adam! You who are capable of constructing Eve from the moonlight! The skulls of those who were here before you gleam all around in the keen moonlight. Behold and consider the wonders and marvel.

How much oil did you pour into the icon lamp?
Are you brave enough to go back?
(And the first cocks crow.)

(1958)

The Lights of the Big City

1

A red streetcar describes two or three red-hot circles, and then it flies down into the river, like a cigarette butt hurled from the bridge.

A jazz trumpet cries out the onset of curfew. The prostitutes race flustered to their hiding places.

A stray dog makes its way down into the toilets. A prostitute who is deaf and dumb barks at the moon. A woman in black slowly leads a white horse to the slaughterhouse.

A boy who has lost his way sleeps under the traffic light in the intersection.

2

People in white hoods squeeze black worms of shoe polish out of an enormous tube and stretch them out across the yellowed teeth of the streets. On the cobblestones squadrons of paper ships sail about with a piece of bloody sanitary pad. Obituaries wither on the tree trunks.

A yellow delivery truck makes a stop at the maternity ward; little white coffins are borne out of it. Another one halts in front of a café, where bullets are unloaded and exchanged for used green shell casings.

Blind sleepwalking women appear from the bars and begin their journeys to the moon.

3

A hen has laid some eggs on a park bench. A rooster comes out from under a sleeping woman's skirt and applauds. The woman, alarmed by his crowing, suffers a miscarriage in the ditch. It's a big blond boy. A taxi driver cuts the umbilical cord and drives on.

A gray dove, frightened by the baby's cries, falls from the roof onto the sidewalk. It drinks avidly from a puddle. Red water lilies shoot up within the outline of the bird's beak. The woman bathes her child in the puddle and tosses him joyfully into the air. An old lady wakes up behind the windowpane and makes threats with her toothless jaws. On the third floor a window is flung open and a pair of white doves comes flying out.

(1959)

Novo Groblje

A woman, naked and touched in the head, prunes the grave-top crosses as she titters wildly. Only a white obelisk remains, jutting up a head taller than the rest. (The madwoman gives it a wide berth.)

Chains rattle on the ankles of the couple entering the chapel at the base of the obelisk. A learned black dog unlocks the padlock on their chains and afterwards sets about eating the steak with mustard that the girl has tossed into a battered helmet for him.

He lights the eternal flame, and she takes off all her clothes. Panting after intercourse, they light cigarettes on the flame and flick the ashes into the eye sockets of a skull, on the vertex of which a heart with dates has been tattooed.

An old woman with a little bell around her neck, singing a lullaby. Another covers a bone with stamps from the old postcards she is reading in the moon's light.

From under a tomb slab comes a gurgling sound, after which a colorful marble made of glass bounces out. A hand, gloved in black lace, picks the marble up and inserts it into the hole again, like in a vending machine. From out of the hole a medallion now appears, no bigger than a finger nail. As if the machine were malfunctioning.

The woman places the medallion under her tongue and walks away.

The gravedigger plucks oakum from the muzzle of a cannon and sticks his head in the barrel. Inside you can hear the sounds of a harmonica. "One, clubs, spades, ace."

The gravedigger is saying something in the barrel as if into a microphone. Then a heavy military-issue boot, shod with nails, lands at his feet; a handful of yellowing dominos comes pouring out of it. He flips over the card that had blown out.

A young man with face paint the color of quicklime, wearing the black mask of a Mardi Gras prince, climbs down from the moon on a liana. He balances on a tightrope strung between crosses, as over nets drying in the light of the moon. A diadem spider dreams of fish; a bat plows into a net at the other end of the cemetery. The spider is startled from his sleep. The young man in the Mardi Gras mask loses his balance and tumbles onto a freshly covered grave and its white roses.

From the burial mound a black cat scurries, carrying the bat between its teeth. The young man runs his fingers over the cat, Witchie, and recognizes her by her hair. He produces a pair of scissors, silver, in order to cut off a lock.

(1959)

Golden Rain

The thing that happened
comes quite close to a miscarriage
in which between intercourse and birth
the borders of time are effaced
and things take place
in impossible simultaneity

the condition of peculiar weakness
and power
and I feel it as
epiphany and as
blasphemy and as
annunciation as
the arrival of someone unknown
as uncertainty itself
as general enervation
and universal strain
as the focal point
where all contradictions
cross
as a golden rain
impregnated by sperm
that is divine

even my friends
value this hour
and they (likely) sense
my power
that's nearly divine
and looking on in fear are
my sister and my
wife
for it probably reminds them
of their miscarriages
and their labor
pains
and so they leave me alone
my wife retreats
into a fertile
ambiguous silence
and my sister goes about on
tip-toes and automatically
brings me a bowl
of tepid water
a little confused and
alarmed
with the justification
after all quite naive
and transparent
that the basin with water
could be of use

if the vertigo should make me start
to vomit
or at least I could moisten my brow
or wash my feet

and perhaps out of all this
that monster was born
(this poem)
because his coming
was not accompanied by
a flash of lightning or the obligatory
scream of maternity or
paternity and not
by a comet either

although the silence
was worthy
of respect

yet what saw the light of day was some
bizarre little freak
my son or father or
brother twin who the hell
knows what
a slimy toad
a ball of snake
blindworm lizard fish

a bloody blob
with no eyes without a face
tadpole
wingless bird
suicide-bird
ejecta of the species
abortion of the blood
abomination of reason not resembling
me in the least but yet
so close to my
blood
conceived in my
consumptive handkerchief
a phenomenon they write about
in medical journals
a monster that one
stores on the shelf
in formaldehyde the fruit of sinful
love of incest
oedipus' seed *in statu nascendi*
fatal flaw of infallible
god beast
of self-exaltation medusa
amoeba unfertilized sputum
self-generating fruit of onanism
agony's embryo hybrid
of black blood
and green herbs

(and it could have been
judging from the harbingers
the song of songs winged
nike, right arm of the venus
di milo the smile of the gioconda
christ moses
god incarnate)

but the fault is mine
for being unable to carry
the fruit even if heavenly
for the 184 days in my blood in
my gut and
what else was there to do
but take the freak
throw it into the toilet and
pull the chain
like it had been
nothing
I guess I'm not crazy and won't
preserve it self-indulgently in
a jar in
some alcohol

(the sin is enough and
so is this poem
and every poem)

my sister clears away the bowl
stony-faced as if
a corpse lay on display
in the house my wife without
a word lays out a white
shirt for me

22.VIII.1961

Anatomy of a Scent

Odoratus impedit cogitationem.
ST. BERNARD

here
is what makes up
a single ounce of perfume
with an imposing name

9,500 jasmine blossoms
of French provenance
4,800 roses
also from France
eighty more roses cruelly slain
by thirst
in the wastelands of Morocco

the flower of one species of iris
which flourishes solely
in estates near Florence
where they've set up
monstrous crematoria and where
and sun-powered ovens are used
to make the blossoms exude
their confessions

lastly thirty-five
factory-made aromatic
chemicals
deployed for the sake of balance
a bit on one side and then the other
to maintain integrity of soul
for each and every flower,
partisan as they are
and intolerant

impregnated by sperm
that is divine

(1962)

Autumn

the wedding celebrations begin
the mating cries of the woodpecker sound
like the pounding of a drum
the art of being liked is endlessly
varied

wild ducks get engaged
in november
it happens that way
so the flocks of travelers
flying from russia and all over
can find their way back
to long-established counterparts
on the same old lakes
of the île de france
tailed by their tragedies
and smut

(1962)

Tropical Nights

1

Whenever the shining moon is absent, the jungles are darker than all other places on earth. Utter gloom prevails. So there are no stars to be seen. And even during the day you cannot always see the sun. Still there are many types of animals living under the vaults of lianas and foliage, animals that are not to be found anywhere else on our planet.

In the night there is silence in the jungles. And yet it teems with life. In the complete darkness little reddish and green and yellow sparks flicker incessantly, ominously.

In the night the time of fangs and claws commences. The time of tragedies.

2

At night the *tamandua*, the golden anteater, awakens. It feeds on termites. The *tamandua* is a close relative of the sloth and can remain fixed to one spot for several days. Woe to whatever it attacks, be it jaguar, howler monkey, or man. In the wink of an eye the *tamandua* pounces on whatever creature is irritating it, taking aim the whole time at the belly of its adversary.

3

All night long the bats are in motion beneath the domes. They annihilate vast quantities of insects. In this regard they are outdone by the vampire bats, which feed on nothing but the blood of birds and animals, along with that of humans. (People in Europe knew nothing of these bloodthirsty animals until the return of Columbus and his companions to Spain.) The vampire bat does not suck out blood; it licks it up with its tongue. Its saliva contains a special substance that prevents the blood from clotting. That's why the wounded victim continues bleeding for hours after the little leech has let him go.

4

At night the ponderous birds known as *guajaros* also go hunting. They are no bigger than ordinary hens and spend their days deep inside spacious caves. As soon as darkness descends, they come out of the cave: first the scouts and after them the remaining birds, in groups of twenty to thirty. In one night these birds can travel up to three hundred kilometers. They fly without any noise at all and get their bearings the same way bats do.

5

In the jungles there are lampions. The brightest among them are the beetles of Puerto Rico. Just two such beetles are capable of illuminating an entire room. In this light, human faces look deathly pale. There are, however, known cases of these beetles saving human lives. During the Spanish-American War, surgery was carried out by the light of these lanterns.

When these lampions are extinguished, it is darker in the jungles than anywhere else in the world.

(1963)

Piano, Out of Tune

along an avenue of black forests rides
an abbess
on her bicycle

a policeman crosses himself
before a cathedral

a cathedral of lace

an old woman who offers love
to anyone for thirty *francs*
plus the room

in a shop on the corner
they sell warm pajamas
and chewing gum
for dogs

a drunken sailor
embracing the street

in a café they're serving
cocoa and bitter liquors

a tall Congolese
dies of public

homesickness
like a kangaroo

the eyes of a nubile waitress
in the café "Italia"
call to mind Modigliani's
women

A German in his cups recalls
a Pole named Maria Kazinska
whom he kissed

in 1943
with one hand
on his pistol
the other on her left breast

an out of tune
piano
reminds me of that safe haven
in Paris
where I shed tears once of an evening
watching a couple
clutch and kiss

Strasbourg

(December 1962)

No Rain Over London

The world has changed too much
No rain over London
The fog will break up
above the capital cities
with their gloom

What we do expect are improvements
in public health
a general offensive
against
cancer

Whales will turn into
domestic livestock
carefully selected and marked
they'll be kept
in
herds

Ninety percent of vices
will disappear

Summer vacation
on the moon

in deep
hotels

People will have complete control
of their nights

The citizens of the USSR will
find in the ocean
all their raw materials

Robots will take the seats
of government ministers

Apollinaire Dreams of Love

Lines written
on soiled scraps of cardboard
on the pages
of calendars
on the cover of a *Mercure de France*

the commander of the 38th regiment's artillery
deep in the forest
waits on answers

new year's day 1915
in the train
between Nice and Marseilles

colossal blue sea,
and a morning full of light
an encounter
before the backdrop of war
rain
and despair

and he's making her
a ring
from a piece of copper

of a German shell
77 caliber

o that distinct image
the power of the spirit
of a Vittoria Colonna
and the mystical fervor
of St. Teresa

war
that naked drama
of ruin
parapets
of living flesh

a redolent angel
hovers
above
the black
fumes

the paper-knife
also made of German
shell casings
a trenchcoat button
like the glittering wing
of a butterfly

and an aromatic angel hovers
above the black
fumes

(1963)

The Fair-haired Girl From Joyce

Recognition of the bold lie and
fires of revolt
and
cherry trees beyond the horizon

A clear night
on the steps
of the streetcar
Verses about the starry
night sky

Slavery
to melancholy

The room of a housemaid
hired from the muddy street
Warm rising and
falling of an exposed
breast

First twilights and
sketchy environs
of the houses of ill repute

Perfumed bodies
along with something else
indeterminate

Senses driven mad
by desire

Lines for the fair-haired
woman
from the steps
of the tram.

(1963)

Garbage Dump

For Leonid Šejka

TIN CANS

Rife shells
fired off at the sun
in vain narcissism

Discarded seashells
worn and rain-etched

stinking fish
with hearts of inserted lemon

The weeds will eat
all of it gradually
even bone and skin

the grass is at its most gluttonous
in graveyards and on
dung-heaps

BOTTLES

1

Bottles drunk
of lavender
of chamomile

bottles with lungs of
lilac

bottles with the soul
of wine

fluted bottles
home to orange slices

2

The wind gets drunk in them
and starts to stumble

or starts to go mad
or poisons itself

or sucks at their nipples
or kisses their lips

or toasts them with blood
or refreshes itself through a straw

or calls down the rains
to drown them

or summons the sun
so they perish of thirst

or invites in the earth
to turn them to green stone

or beckons to the moon
to smash them up

to toss them into the stream
like little broken mirrors

GENESIS

1

First born is the grub
then the butterfly and
then the worm

then the mosquito and
the fly and
the bumblebee

and the bumblebee begets
the dung beetle

and the dung beetle
the dragonfly

and on the seventh day out of the rubbish pile flies
a bird

2

it spits down on the earth
on the grass
and on the ants

and that's why the grass
now invests the bird's head

and why the ants
luxuriate on its bones

the reason the earth swindles it

become sky, it
reddens the bird's beak with blood.

SHOES

1

thank God
on the midden-heap
we're all the same

don't lie and tell us your mother
was a serpent

mine was
an ordinary
swine

and you didn't break the heel of your shoe at a ball
you stepped on shit instead

besides
you will see after the first rain
or when the thaw begins

your own dear mother
wouldn't even recognize you

2

nothing will remain
of these rigged scales
after the deluge begins

and no radiant days
till the coming of may

the rains will come
and piss on you some
and put out both your eyes

the grass will come
and run you through
lull you to sleep

and kids will come
to yank out your tongue
and drill into your ears

but pray to god
some roma come around
and heal you with a song

so you can dance a bit more
in the middle of the mud
with teeth made of gold

until you leave
the violets calm

REFRAIN

Blessed are the tramps
blessed are the gypsies
for they shall find a coin of gold

blessed are the children
    (woe to the children)
awaiting their sure case
of melancholy

(1963-1970)

Still Life with Fish

A candle like an x-ray: ribs.
Candlestick: cathedral of silver.

A bloody piece of liver quivers on porcelain.
Sturgeons exhaling through salted wounds.

Yellow of lemon, fragrant skin.
White plate rim. The gleam of a knife.

Like liquid rubber the cheese pours.
Biblical peace of carmen apples.

In the mirror the room's double trembles.
On the flame of the candle a moth alights.

(1966)

Garbage Dump

Refuse of humans and of animals: fingernails, hair
Women's hair that crackled under the
    electric touch of a comb
Mica-like corns shorn with a razor blade
Dark lichen of wounds
Hairs from a leg from a nose from an ear
Fragrant moss of female armpits
A fish skull
Broadened fans of turnips,
The double-edged combs of fish backbones,
Scalded pullet heads,
Wet black feathers,
Clenched chicken legs with waxen scales,
Animal bones all the marrow sucked out,
Green chicken guts tied in a knot
Tubes of fish bones resembling cross-stitch patterns,
Double-ballooned fish bladders
Apple scraps
Pits stones seeds of plums of peaches of watermelons
Sour cherry pits like vitamins
Crumpled and cipher-scrawled carbon paper
Rotten fruit with maggots eating its flesh
    as though it were human

Chewed-up cigarette holders of cherrywood
    and rubber and amber
Cigarette holders like yellow fingers
Blue razor blades, blue envelopes for razor blades,
    streetcar tickets, labels
Paper lace from teletype tape
Remnants of lace that's been starched
Gold tubes of emptied lipstick like rifle shell casings
Shells of eggs from which billed monsters
    have hatched devoid of wings and tails
Beer bottle caps
Tiles from busted flower pots
Reeds, rotting straw,
The black banner of an umbrella
A parasol's birdlike skeleton
Napkins displaying the death mask of lips
Empty paper bags protecting in their folds
    grains of crystal like in the soft flesh of a conch
A sliced carrot with the rings at its center
    green and then redder and redder
Husks from beans like amputated lips
Burnt-out light bulbs like eggs of the Firebird (fire-wires)
Membership cards with their ten commandments
    nobody believes in anymore
Yellowed handcuffs
Silk neckties like plucked stalks of water-flowers

Tubes of toothpaste pressed clean
Corks,
Photography done in the moonshine
Carnations in hideous decay
Tulips narcissuses gladioli
Lillies giving the rubbish heap the appearance of a graveyard
Nails paperclips thumbtacks needles screws hairpins
Reddish curls of copper wire
Pens all used up
    Cobwebs of nylon stockings
Gloves without mates
Strings of stove burners
Old shoes on their slow way to becoming green as grass
Children's drawings of sun and sky to which rain has added
    its signature, transforming them into masterpieces
Garish dust jackets of books like the bloody uterus
    of poetry's muses
Ladies' hairpins with beaks misaligned like that of a parrot
Pickled strips of crepe paper
Rusty wires
The lacy shavings from sharpened pencils
Walnut shells like sprung bird skulls
Decayed marrow from walnuts akin to human brains
Little tubes of straw and their rolled-down socks of cigarette paper
Toothbrushes, with nothing but roots remaining in gums of glass
Tin crates, cardboard boxes
Glass test tubes with aspirin lying in them like ripe peas

Bottles for milk beer Coca-Cola
bottles with tiny mouths like leeches
bottles zurlas flutes ocarinas
bottles with busted bellies like fish
bottles with green lacerations
bottles that reek of marc and throw-up
bottles with apple stoppers in their snouts
    like a slaughtered suckling pig
bottles with inksplotched mouths like the mouths
    of gradeschool pupils
orange peels like a woman's skin between the shoulder blades
orange peels with lining like that of leather gloves
crusts of bread souring in dirty water like in an old man's
    toothless mouth
squeezed-out hemispheres of lemon
spiral coils of apple skins
watermelon rinds like fresh horsemeat beset by blackflies
banana peels looking like flayed male members
potato peelings hewn simply, luxuriantly, like slices of bread
Brown tufts of dust
Cigarette ash
Wrung-out butts resembling great white maggots that have
    hatched out this heap
Condoms, slimy bags in which homunculi decay
The wavy porcelain of smashed plates
Crumpled newspapers running late by at least a fortnight
Plastic, plexiglass

Cotton clumps with coagulated blood and pus
Buttons made of antler tin mother-of-pearl
Pieces of gauze straight out of an embroidery frame
Sanitary napkins displaying blooming womanhood
Bandages with golden hairs stuck behind with their white roots
Poems (including this one)
Envelopes with pulled purple entrails
Stamps red yellow blue green
stamps on which the busts of statesmen poets and conquerors
    of the universe preen
stamps taken prisoner by the touch of a tongue, the way lovers
    imprison one another
stamps over which philatelists go mad, ready to embalm them
stamps branded like cattle
stamps fringed in lace
stamps on which flowers blossom and lions growl
stamps with seals of cities
stamps with dates like on bottles of pasteurized milk so
    the garbage heap might always be fresh
Letters written on knees in trains
letters written on big typewriters by the slender fingers of typists,
    by fingers from which she just licked butter
letters written in a child's hand
letters written in an old man's trembling grip
postcards penned in ballpoint on the terraces of cafés
letters on the letterhead of famous hotels
love letters that the rain has turned to tragedy

Notebooks from gradeschool that should be saved for old
    age
Death notices about which there's nothing to say
Lettuce green cabbage vegetables periwinkle
Dill black pepper carnations cauliflower
Apple scraps (once more)
Clusters of lilac blooms falling gloriously apart like excised
    lungs from a smoker
Rags rubberbands collars
Oilcloths muslin shawls silk
Roses
roses that suit the garbage dump fabulously the same way
    poems do
roses that are starting to stink like people
roses with flies settling on them
roses that the damp hands of a saleswoman once wrapped
    in crinkly thin paper
roses kept in crystal vases like golden fish
roses that had their water changed like a compress on a
    sick person's brow
roses bound in wire like criminals
roses with joints like the joints of an ungulate
roses with leaves so very similar to artificial ones
roses that made me rise at 3:30 in the morning so I would
    not forget them before tomorrow

(1966)

The Poet of the Revolution on Board the Presidential Ship[1]

1. *Protocol*

Thirty white shirts
(three units per day, every day).
Not so you won't be naked,
 just what protocol requires.

Underwear: we won't go there.
(But the Protocol Section will pay, from the tie-clip to the undies.
Your salary is way too low for this.)

As for that tie—
(by the way, you aren't too crazy about Croats, they say)[2]
the cravat, it must match your suit.
Protocol demands this.

Do you have adequate bathing suits
for the beach?
Let's go with ten.
(And don't let them be the ones known as "minis.")

Where you people live,
so it seems anyway,

the custom is to swim
in one's skivvies—
the same ones one wears all the time.

And (just this one thing more about drawers):
do change those things more frequently,
especially if you're attending a reception.
(Don't you call it a "receiver" instead
there in your neck of the woods,
in Srem or Šumadija or whatever?)[3]

Don't shake His hand too much.
And avoid coarse language, the kind you find
in the books by Vuk[4].

And here are a few more words of advice
(stick to them like an oath):
you're not allowed to spit,
and not just not on deck
(that much must be obvious even to you),
but not into the sea either,
and not into the depths of the ocean
even if the weather's gorgeous
because here one must—apart from all considerations of courtesy—
reckon with the power of the winds
(comprising several hundred meters per second).

You will have lackeys and secretaries,
and your own (*en suite*) toilet and shower.
Do shower at least three times a day.

Pertaining to conversation:
it should be (for the most part) light.
With the maximum possible number of anecdotes from the NOB[5]
(and here and there a couple in peasant *moba*[6] style)
and some from Drvar and Vis[7] while we're at it.

Do not dip into the turbid water of nationalism.
Safeguard that old unity-and-brotherhood thing[8];
it's our greatest treasure.

By no means even mention
Djilas, Dedijer, Hebrang.[9]
Don't forget your place.

With Stalin: proceed with caution.
Refer to Trotsky with a scornful smile.
And don't spout about the living.
(In politics everything changes from day to day.)

As pertains to public opinion,
that is your domain:
newspapers, radio, the rest of the press.
You'll be giving your "copy" to me.

Not for the sake of control,
but just to check the spelling.
At least in the case of the "ijekavian" versions
and whatever's written in *latinica*.[10]

Guard everything like it was the strictest (state) secret,
the apple of your eye.
And so: not a whit of private gossip
from our prominent and esteemed—etcetera—
correspondents.

We want no private notes,
no personal opinions,
not a single indiscretion.

Everything that's overly personal
is out of bounds here.

Everything relating to one's own point of view
should in principle
be avoided.

Describe, using plenty of epithets,
only His stance,
comportment,
voice,
and eyes

while He strolls the deck.
Or maybe His hands.
The waves on the ocean,
our ship scudding through them.
Nights in the tropics.
Gulls of the sea.
Stars in the firmament at night.
Nautical engines throbbing full-tilt.

And Him on the deck, at the bow.
Our tricolor—with the Red Star—as it waves.
And a wave as it thuds
against the hull of the ship.

As for drinking,
you're allowed to partake in moderation.
But always take your seat after He does,
and stand up only after Him.

Eat politely, following protocol,
and to the accompaniment of an anecdote or fable—
be it about dogs, wolves, or a falcon.

Owing to this tropical heat
you'll have to take in plenty of fluids.
And for the sake of your voice
as much juice as possible: orange, pineapple,
lots of lemonade.

The poetic soul itself
is not immune to the bottle-squad.
We're all human after all,
and that includes the poets.

So you don't do the poetry thing then?
And you don't go in for spirits?
You'll still need a spot of whiskey with ice.
Trust me. It won't be that hard to swallow.

In your dispatches
(need I even say this?)
not a word about it
(about the drinking or our other little plans).

Stick to business
around the staff
and with the sailors.
Nothing personal.

No questions like:
"Where you from, friend?"
(Or things like this:)
"How long till your tour of duty's up?"
And do not ply the sailors
with alcohol or juice.

Now what about serious literature?
No need to delve into examples here.
Simply put:
narrate crisply and keep your touch light.

Quote the Marxist classics
without kissing their asses
and, to be sure,
writers from our war.
Ćopić is OK to cite but, there
too, take it easy when praising him.

Surely, you know "Majka Knežopoljka"[11] by heart.
Great. Recite it.
Refer to Gorky, the more the better!

Regarding your personal reading material:
don't give it a second thought.
There's a library on board
with plenty of books

from every possible field:
literature, painting, geography, revolutionary history,
poetry anthologies, Marxist studies,
the origins of popular rule,
cookbooks.

Your books are there, too,
definitely,
underlined in various colors
of red and blue and green
(precisely according to the legend we've ratified).

So when He picks them up,
He can form an objective opinion of them
effortlessly,
in passing
on the fly.

I have the impression
your books did not cause Him
too much grief; therefore,
accept my congratulations.

Do you have any other questions?

Oh yes. About crabs and oysters,
(He loves to eat them!)
you must proceed with caution.
It's a science unto itself,
the sort of thing you have to practice at home,
under the expert supervision
of one of our boys.

The items here are all fresh, all the time,
And therefore there's no need to fear food poisoning or dyspepsia.
So, anyway, how are you with parlor games?
Chess, poker, billiards, checkers, and canasta?

Unfortunately the ship isn't the place
for a quick soccer match
(although he went in for that, too,
and successfully, when he was younger
and when there was enough of his valuable time to go around).

Chess is OK. It's already on the agenda.
Are you ranked?
You're not?
But not some kind of moron, right?
So, I repeat, play without any dazzling combinations.
Use classical openings,
G-4, F-4, and such-like,
Don't attack his queen too often
and don't place his king in a hopeless situation,
or tire your knights out
or send your rooks off to where they don't belong.
Stick with your pawns as much as you can—

but just don't play like a school kid.

The pauses between your moves
shouldn't last all too long.
His time is precious!

Conversation at the board
should revolve primarily
around sports or chess.[12]

While you're there, you can mention Nasser,
the Negus, the Shah of Iran, and what-not.

Watch out when you're playing cards—
no joking is allowed in card games.
You'll cover your losses from your own pocket
(except in the case of a major loss, an excessive one, that is).

Here a bitter and uneven battle is also being waged,
you know.

The relationship is unequal:
on the one hand, Him,
whose thoughts are wrapped up in momentous events
(only His hands take part in the game):
His mind is off in India
Iran Russia Africa
amidst the snowy Tatras.

And you?
With your whole being,
all your thoughts—
like you're waiting in ambush—
in those cards.

Kiss the ladies' hands.
If they're really ladies.
The men get called mister and sir;
it's not rocket science.

Comrade and *tovarishch* are only for members of friendly parties
from the Eastern Bloc.
Everything's been written out for you,
so bone up.
Nothing can be allowed to go awry.

All right, now...
You have to know how to dance.
You'll get an instructor:
English waltz, the Viennese, the tango.
You can always use them out there in the wide world.

Keep your hands clasped gently around the waist.
In a dance
the important work falls to the legs,
but "wham-bang-yessirree" hands also play a role!

You have to get your teeth fixed—
there's plenty of time
and we have the best dentists (tooth-bullers!).[13]
If after that
your breath is still skunky,
start using mouthwash.
You only have to do it
when you get up in the morning;
slam it down
on an empty stomach.

The same thing applies to your feet.
Change those socks two or three times a day
and make good use of the shower-spray.

Lose the dandruff.
(And trim the hair a bit, too.)
You'll have to break that habit of
digging in your ears
and picking your nose.
From the orderly you'll receive two or three cans of deodorant—
for use under your arms.

In a word: pay as much attention
to hygiene as you can.

Come back tomorrow at the same time.
And now here is your list.

And one more official request:

Go to our tailor
and he'll let you have it—your sizes, I mean.[14]

I wish you luck and hope for the best,
for you and your pen![15]

There's no reason to waste our breath
on more of this—
it's simple, man.
The decorum in finer society
does not include rooting around in your own nose
or
as they say out there by yours,
over Čačak way—
your nose ain't allowed to be picked.

And one more little
point of etiquette:
it's prohibited…
(um, I said it already, but no matter)
… to spit, whether, as they say, "on the ground,"
or from the deck into the water
or from one side of the ship to the other.

And, another wee example:
no combing your hair at the table.

Just imagine:
a hair—in the sauce!

Yes, well, for today, just one thing more:
from time to time
owing to the heat and perspiration,
your underwear will want to get stuck
between your butt cheeks
and that can really vex a body.

The point is
you may not solve this problem—
absolutely not, not in under any circumstances—
with your paw!
But of course you also may not
laugh too loud.
I mean—
so that we're on the same page here—
you may laugh obligingly
if what's in play
is a joke
by an esteemed...
and so on.
But that does not mean
your mucus has to roll,
or, as the vernacular would have it,
you snot yourself.

If He should broach a new subject,
then that's cause to consider
if the issue is serious,
or if it's all a farce,
on the part of our respected...
and so on.

High-ranking guests
enjoy kidding around,
especially if they're from the Eastern Bloc.
Apropos Eastern Bloc,
it's all really simple actually
but there are a few things worth knowing:

Comrades from the East
kiss on the lips when greeting;
it's like it's written into their Constitution.
The Nonaligned ones
hug each other and swarm about when meeting
The Westerners are on the exterior
very starchy
as if they've swallowed a pole
(that's according to a joking Comrade Dolanc).[16]
They never draw too close to the common folk
nor to the leadership
but they extend their hands
(and they're all the same).
And then they pull them back
like someone's gonna bite them off.

Well, none of this bit applies to you.
These are their internal relations,
but in diplomacy,
especially when it is still young,
born just yesterday, so to speak,
a person has to study for a long time.
(You know what Lenin said about it.)
... So there you have it.

A person must work a little harder
to be a worthy rep
of his country
and the nation.
For various machinations are really possible here.

Let's say some Russian
stuffs his big old tongue in your mouth
(to use the vulgar folksy phrase)
—what do you do, then?
You do the same thing right back to him!
If he squeezes your hand till the bones shatter?
Same thing right back, to be sure.
As they say: an eye for an eye
and a tooth for a tooth;
well, penetration for penetration,
firm grip for firm grip.

Or, for instance,
some Brit (let us say) asks:
"Hau du yu du?"
How do you answer that?
Aha! You see, there is no answer;
there's the rub!
You say the same thing back to him:
"Hau du yu du?"
which is not the way some of our people greet—
they start cursing when they meet.
"What's up, asshole?"

But to move on, to the subject of the winds
(and here I do not have the trade winds in mind),
you simply have to harness those bowels.
(It's like the way the urge can strike you
to open your mouth and yawn,
nodding around the campfire towards dawn.)
Consequently: never fart out loud
or let one sneak out,
actions that become the center of attention
when the matter is one of taste.
Worse than sound is: "Who spread that smell around?"
The best thing, if there's no other recourse,
is to go discreetly outside.
And stay there, the longer the better,
not like some scoundrels who pass gas outside

and immediately return
(or by comparison who
release the dove here
and then head to the deck.)

Easy now, easy. Just take it easy.

(No, this is not a quote from Lenin.
It's a paraphrase.)

The path here will take you right up to the road
and that is where
your limousine awaits.

(Over his shoulder, melancholy, as he walks along
the graveled path towards home:)

The leaves have fallen;
it soon will be winter;
and He loves the temperate zones.

(1988)

NOTES

[1] The original of this poem, "Pesnik revolucije na predsedničkom brodu," is well known in the former Yugoslavia. The subject is the clique around Yugoslav leader Josip Broz Tito (1892-1980), who was fond of sea voyages on his "floating residence," the naval vessel *Galeb* ("Seagull"). Some historians maintain that the poem is a broadside aimed at the Serbian writer Dobrica Ćosić, who had been close to Tito and traveled with him in the 1960s prior to becoming a Serbian nationalist who enjoyed a reputation as a dissident. Others interpret the Serbian-Croatian tensions lampooned in the piece as evidence that a kind of Croatian inner circle controlled access to the leader. Tito is the godlike "He" of the poem. As this is the longest and most overtly political work in Kiš's small poetic oeuvre, we include translator's notes for a number of key references here.

[2] *Croats, they say*: Here Kiš makes use of a typical pun: the word for tie (*kravata*) is juxtaposed to the word for Croat (*hrvat*), with the understanding that this similarity exists in many European languages and that the ethnic term likely relates to the derivation of the article of clothing.

[3] *...in Srem or Šumadija...*: Regions in former Yugoslavia. The narrator is referring to pronunciation differences

between Serbian and Croatian. A common difference is the existence of the infix "ije" in many Croatian words. For instance, Croatian for milk is most commonly *mlijeko* while in Serbian it is *mleko*. Likewise Croatian inhabitants of the province of Srem would call the region Srijem. The joke therefore is that the word "reception" in this stanza exists only as *prijem*, a word that seems to follow the Croatian pattern but in actuality derives from another source. The narrator's patronizing attitude leads him to invent a Serbian variant that does not actually exist, *prem*.

[4] Vuk Karadžić (1787-1864) was a famous Serbian scholar who published a dictionary, grammar, and several collections of Serbian folk poems.

[5] NOB is the Serbo-Croatian acronym for World War II in Yugoslavia. More specifically, the term *Narodnooslobodilačka borba* ("National Liberation Struggle") refers to the war of Tito's Communist-led Partisan forces against the Axis occupiers (the armed forces of Germany, Italy, Hungary, and Bulgaria) and domestic collaborators or anti-Partisans (the Croatian Ustaše, the Serbian Chetniks, and others).

[6] *moba*: a traditional communal work effort, akin to a barn-raising or sewing bee, among peasants in Southeastern Europe.

[7] *Drvar and Vis*: These place names refer to sites of famous actions in World War II. Drvar is a town in Bosnia where Tito almost fell into the hands of German paratroops in 1944. Vis is the remote island in the Adriatic to which Tito fled after the attack on Drvar and which he used as his base of operations for the subsequent unification of Yugoslavia.

[8] *...that old unity-and-brotherhood thing*: The folksy tone and slang of this stanza serve to undermine the gravity of the concept of *bratstvo i jedinstvo* ("Brotherhood and Unity"), the nationality policy of socialist Yugoslavia. Tito and the League of Communists of Yugoslavia actively propagated "Brotherhood and Unity" among Serbs, Croats, Slovenes, Bosnians, Kosovar Albanians, Macedonians, and the many other population groups as the solution to the country's long-standing ethnic rivalries and recent intercommunal bloodshed. Among other flourishes, the order of the two elements of the concept is reversed.

[9] *Djilas, Dedijer, Hebrang*: Milovan Djilas, Vladimir Dedijer, and Andrija Hebrang were, respectively, Montenegrin, Serbian, and Croatian Communists who, for various reasons, fell out of favor with the post-war Yugoslav regime.

[10]   *"ijekavian" and latinica*: These are linguistic terms that apply to the Croatian language (or, as one would have more likely said in Kiš's day, to the Croatian variant of the Serbo-Croatian language). As discussed in Note 3 above, Croatian words often have an extra syllable ("ije") in the middle where Serbian words have a simple "e"; hence the designation of the main dialect among Croats as "ijekavian." *Latinica* is simply the modified Latin alphabet used by Croats (and by many other Slavs, such as Slovenes, Czechs, and Poles), as opposed to the *ćirilica*, or Cyrillic alphabet, used by Serbs, Russians, Bulgarians, and others.

[11]   *"Majka Knežopoljka"*: A reference to a long revolutionary poem by the Bosnian writer Skender Kulenović (1910-1978). The work's full title was "Stojanka majka knežopoljka" (Eng. "Stojanka, the Mother from Knežopolje"). The poem, written in 1942 amidst the brutal Axis occupation of the country and the ensuing civil war, became a Partisan classic.

[12]   *around sports or chess*: The use of the word for "chess," *šah*, here sets up a joke in the form of a homophone completed in the next stanza with the appearance of the Serbo-Croatian word for "Shah," *Šah*.

¹³ *tooth-bullers*: Here Kiš has added a synonym for dentist in parentheses. This additional word, *zubar*, is the traditional word for "dentist" but also means "buffalo." Again, humor is the main purpose of this apposition, but it also implies that the dentist is a brute or that the unsophisticated listeners (presumably accomplished journalists but all with little experience in personal hygiene) might not understand the newer word, *dentista*.

¹⁴ *your sizes, I mean*: The verbal phrase used in this sentence, *uzmiti meru*, means both "to take someone's measurements" (as in a tailor's shop) and "to kick someone's ass" (as in a fight). The whole protocol session depicted in this poem is a roughing-up, an enforcement of conformity (with the carrots of temporary luxury and proximity to the dictator); the hypothetical tailor may be a Party thug also, or simply an unfortunate intermediate target for Kiš's humor.

¹⁵ *for you and your pen*: The operative idiom in the source means the same as "to keep one's fingers crossed" in English. But the image of "holding [up] one's fist" also denotes the Communist Party's salute in the era of the Spanish Civil War, in which many Yugoslav Communists took part. This denotation of solidarity or collusion within the ambit of the Party is paralleled by a tertiary possible interpretation: a threat in the form of a shaking fist.

[16] *Comrade Dolanc*: Stane Dolanc (1925-1999) was a Slovene politician close to Tito. He was known as a political heavyweight and a hard-liner in the League of Communists of Yugoslavia. The sarcastic reference is underscored by a pun on the Serbo-Croatian word *kolac* (pole), which is rendered as the dialectally-tinged *kolanc* to rhyme with his name. Another meaning of *kolac* is stake, as in the apparatus for impalement under the Ottomans.

News of the Death of Mrs. M.T.

It's a job well done, Death;
what a success
at wrecking a fortress like that!
To wolf down so much meat,
to crack that many bones
in such a short time.
Using up energy, so much,
so fast, like a burning cigarette.
What labor that must have been, Death,
what a demonstration of might.
(As if we could have failed
to take you at your word.)

(1989)

The Man Who Wrote the World: Danilo Kiš and Poetry

My brain hurt like a warehouse,
it had no room to spare,
I had to cram so many things,
to store everything in there.

David Bowie, "Five Years" (1972)

The Danilo Kiš of the great novels *Garden, Ashes* (1965) and *Hourglass* (1972), that same insistent but cool impresario of the immortal cycle of stories in *A Tomb for Boris Davidovich* (1976), is happily recognizable in a number of the poems in this modest collection. His veteran readers will see in "Biography" and "A Jewish Girl, a Poem" tender parallels to his autobiographical prose, an intensely personal journey into the Central Europe of the Holocaust; those experienced readers might also want to recommend these same poems to new readers of Kiš as a short but effective overture. It was in the hope of offering fuller insights into Kiš's fictional world, autobiography, and creative process that I decided upon the translation of these poems.

Danilo Kiš: Biographical Notes

Danilo Kiš (1935-1989), native son of the flat, fertile multicultural border region of Vojvodina between Serbia and Hungary and commonly hailed as one of the greatest, if not the greatest, Serbian writers of all time; Kiš, heir to a welter of legacies including his Montenegrin mother's proud Balkan autodidacticism and robust love of challenge along with his father's Hungarian-Jewish intellectualism and sense of peril, prey to (or beneficiary of) a strong case of wanderlust and an almost innate identification with the values of modernism and revolution; Kiš, who wrote his earliest poems in Hungarian and was devoted to the verse of Endre Ady, Anna Akhmatova, and the French Symbolists, and who embraced at once cosmopolitanism and a deep and abiding love for the specificities of his chief language (Serbo-Croatian or Serbian);

this Kiš was a dogged defender of human rights and human dignity, a fearlessly keen but indefatigably sensitive observer of detail, a pioneer in the laboratory of form, and an accomplished and prolific translator from French, Russian, Hungarian, and other languages. And this Kiš is still very much with us, in relevance and in popularity, as recent nonfiction works by Milan Kundera (*The Curtain*, 2006) and Andrzej Stasiuk (*Fado*, 2009) attest.

Born in Subotica, in northern Yugoslavia, on October 15, 1935, Kiš and some members of his family survived World War II by living in rural obscurity in southwestern Hungary. After the war, he spent many of his teen years in Montenegro with the maternal side of his family and then studied literature at the University of Belgrade. He rapidly became an active participant in a number of intellectual circles; over the course of his career he wrote poetry, short stories, novels, screenplays, dramas, polemics, and a large number of literary and cultural essays. Linking all his works is an intense preoccupation with the "other," people who are marginalized and exposed to perils of many sorts, most notably deep humiliation and annihilation. He underscored time and again his opposition to authoritarianism and "group-think" (in its political, ethnic, and literary variants), but he was also an untiring proponent of formal experimentation and of the recognition of art's necessity, as art, in our creative and moral life. Above all, Kiš paid attention to process and resisted the instrumentalization of art; his outstanding works continue to direct readers' attention to both the emotions and ethics of history.

Selection Criteria and Methodology

These translations account for well over half of Kiš's poetic oeuvre. The reasons behind a translator's or editor's selections always vary, but it is only fair, to casual readers and scholars alike, to include them. Here I have not included all of his homages to James Joyce, because of their very specific nature, nor any of his "word play" poems (untranslatable soundscapes, really—wild and willful polyglot flurries of words that take rhyme, assonance, and alliteration to sometimes inscrutable extremes) or of his long epigraphs that read like poems. Almost all the lyric poetry is here, along with all five of his rich prose poems that in some ways read like his rich prose. His long, hilarious, caustic and supremely political satire "The Poet of the Revolution on Board the Presidential Ship" is included in this volume as well, because Kiš's occasional disavowal of politics was misleading, although his rejection of political parties and ideology was far from disingenuous. Indeed Kiš was a supremely political figure, and a political thinker, in his lifetime, and a small personal echo—for the doggedly historical among us—of that trait can be found here in "Wedding Guests," a metaphor akin to the neckties of various colors in Kiš's play *Night and Fog*, pointing to political stripes and pointing out the people who simply suffer from politics.

A few notes on the sources and texts of these poems are in order. The English translations have been prepared on the basis of the volume of Kiš's collected works entitled *Pesme, Elektra* (ed. Mirjana Miočinović and published in 1995 by BIGZ in Beograd). Kiš usually employed free verse; I have done so in all of the translations, maintaining line breaks as much as possible and syntax allowing, in order to focus on diction, emotions and ideas. When the original contains a notation of the location in which it was written, I have included that notation in italics under the translation. Also at the bottom of each item is the date of composition, derived either from Kiš's own annotation or from notes in the Miočinović volume. The poems are organized chronologically, though one may think of them as falling into three categories—lyric, political, and prose. Such a division, however, is not definitive in terms of the author's overall poetic output, nor is it the preferred organizational tool for tracking Kiš's development as a writer.

Kiš and Translation

Kiš was a prolific translator, especially of poetry, his whole life. To some extent he viewed translation as a kind of equalizer, a mechanism—almost a service—whereby important poetic works from "minor languages" could circulate in the larger world. But this accounts for only some of his voluminous translations, the Hungarian works, for instance. Above all, however, Kiš translated from Russian and French into Serbian, so with these "major languages" something different is at work. It was, in part, an effort to familiarize his fellow Yugoslavs with international authors he valued highly; it was also a way to help make a living.

But there is more, of course. Kiš let it be known, eloquently but hardly obliquely, that translating verse was great practice for writing poetry or, to refer to the discussion in the preceding section of this afterword, to develop the poetic in himself as a writer. Ultimately, though, translation for Kiš was a labor of love, or, as he put it, consolation, a way of cultivating a deep relationship with a work of art he adored.

He published his translations in journals and in book form. A cross-section of poetry that he translated reveals his theoretical and cultural preoccupations. From Russia there were Anna Akhmatova, Marina Tsvetaeva, Osip Mandelstam, and Sergei Yesenin; from Hungary there were Ady, Attila József, Ferenc Juhász, Agnes Nemes-Nagy, Sándor Petőfi, György Petri, Miklós Radnóti, and Ottó Tolnai; and from France there were Guillaume Apollinaire, Baudelaire, Comte de Lautréamont, Jacques Prévert, Raymond Queneau, and Paul Verlaine. The list reads like a *Who's Who* of modern literature. Indeed Kiš rendered into Serbo-Croatian many poems by each of these writers, as well as verse by an almost inexhaustible list of other writers from these time periods. He even compiled anthologies, such as one in the 1960s featuring translated works from wartime Vietnam, and another in the 1980s, the translated title of which elicits a wry smile from Kiš fans who have already discovered the sense of humor tucked away in some of his essays: *The Muses' Bordello: An Anthology of French Erotic Poetry.*

Kiš and Poetry

When Danilo Kiš discussed, as he frequently did, his influences and inspirations, he tended to mention fiction writers. From his fellow Yugoslavs Ivo Andrić and Miroslav Krleža, to the Russians Boris Pilnyak and Isaac Babel, and then Borges, Joyce, and, perhaps looming unexpectedly sovereign over them all, Rabelais. Yet Kiš also talked about poetry often, and, to judge from the number of references and the tone of near-veneration, there was no writer he actively admired more than Charles Baudelaire, above all for his revolutions of subject matter and expressiveness. On a related note, he several times noted wistfully that he might have written more poetry had not Endre Ady, whose works deeply enchanted him as a young man, not already said much of what he wished to say.

Kiš's deep love for poetry manifested itself in his frequent praise and citation of poets he respected, and in his years of work as a prolific translator; he wrote a number of essays on specific poets or poems, above all, Hungarians. But in two other ways, Kiš's love for poetry was less obvious but can still be gleaned from his essays and interviews. It's apparent that he often used poetry as a synonym for "literature" in general. And literature is great and necessary because it embraces doubt, especially in the face of ideology, and because it gives emotion and individual sensibility to history. Kiš even went so far as to say that poetry corrects the indifference and futility of existence because it embraces memory and works against relativism and death.

The final facet of this embrace of poetry is what one might refer to as "the poetic." He saw poetry as a creative activity that was especially independent, personal, and driven to the point of obsession. It was a privileged mode of work for experimentation, and he felt that the combination of poetic compulsion and lyricism was the main force propelling the development of his prose style. Thus we have *homo poeticus*—a term on display in the titles of one of Kiš's books and also of one of his greatest essays. For Kiš this term denoted the feeling, thinking, inventing writer. When he referred to himself as a *poète manqué*, more was at work than just modesty or self-deprecation. This was the embodiment of the author's realization that he was called, inexorably, to prose for his fullest artistic development, but that he would always rely on the methods and inspirations of great poets.

Kiš did not always think highly of his own poetry, and he did not write a great deal of it. Most of it belongs to the domains of the "early" and "experimental." It is, therefore, obvious and noteworthy that poetry and the poetic were of disproportionately great significance to his vocation.

Some Thoughts on These Poems

Translators read deeply, and repeatedly, and we've also been known to sing and whisper and shout and otherwise declaim or even dance to works that we are translating, especially poetry, especially when we think no one's looking. This doesn't make translators, especially when they are historians like the author of this afterword, into anything approaching an authoritative arbiter of literary taste, but in the interests of sparking engaged reading and perhaps continued discussion, this might be an appropriate place to say a few words about a few of the poems that are particularly striking or moving, at least to me.

It's hard to imagine anything more quintessentially Danilo Kiš than the opening poem, "Biography." This is especially true for people like me, who to came to Kiš first by means of his autobiographical prose. It is a frank and painfully lyrical evocation of his father's own youth and ultimate fate; it skips, except for some broad strokes, Eduard's troubled and conflicted adulthood, and in that way, it complements the picture of Kiš's family that readers of his prose may have already put together.

The next two poems, "Sunset" and "Anatomy of a Scent," reflect a sense of planning and priority that later showed up in Kiš"'s stories and novels. He takes a powerful sensory impression, one visual and one olfactory, and breaks them down into their constituent parts, mixing them with muted images of violence and with geographic references suggestive of some kind of incantation or would-be omniscience. Their combined effect is powerful, and repeated readings bring out differing nuances and details.

"Golden Rain," intriguing as it is, seems almost *sui generis* to this observer, and perhaps uncharacteristically solipsistic. Meanwhile, a large subset of the poems in this volume is built from juxtaposing disparate images around a loosely defined theme. The World War I poem about Apollinaire, along with the two piano poems, is a compound of carnage and quiet symbols of love and artistic endurance; the exquisite still lifes are animated, to a considerable degree, by careful diction and words connected to motion; and "No Rain over London" and "The Fair-haired Girl from Joyce" employ their stores of images for very different ends, the first being fantastic and sarcastic, and the second delicately descriptive.

The two poems entitled "Garbage Dump" are perhaps the most indispensable poems in this book. They are the product of Kiš at the peak of his powers of enumeration, a method he often employed in his novels, either gently, to preserve in words some of the elements of a Central European world lost in World War II, or remorselessly, to catalog atrocities committed by the Axis during World War II. It is also an example of the minute examination of reality that Kiš practiced in some of his stories and that he advocated as a way of assembling art from real, refracted, observable, "true" things around him.

Kiš often commented in interviews on the nature of reality as opposed to fictional settings or assemblages of material things in his works. Scholars have also studied his practices of enumeration; these practices had many causes, or aims, but, in their desire to delineate or notate a lost world, they bear some resemblance to techniques used by the Croatian novelist Miroslav Krleža. The epigraph to this essay, from a song by David Bowie, illustrates the modern impulse to store and warehouse and find room in our brains for observed reality. In fact, another David Bowie motif, about searching "for form and land" (from "The Man Who Sold the World") illustrates a related drive that Kiš expressed forcefully at the end of his novel Mansarda: to give shape, emotionally and artistically, to what he as author was processing cognitively.

Among the many poems here that treat of death, familial suffering, and loss, "Wedding Guests" stands out because of its simple political or historical message. At this poem's heart is the equivalence, or equation via suffering, of the two sides in the civil war in Yugoslavia. By easy extension it also equates the villains who carried out Axis aggression and the other, later ones who subjugated Eastern Europe in the name of Stalinism. Indeed, Kiš wrote against what he would call "totalitarianism," of both the left and the right, for the whole of his adult life. Kiš's apolitical imagery is also fresh and striking, especially in "Autumn" and "News of the Death of Mrs. M.T."

The author's sprawling political satire, "The Poet of the Revolution on Board the Presidential Ship," is positively Rabelaisian in its scope and humor. Although a significant number of footnotes are required to make much of it intelligible to a non-Yugoslav audience, it deserves to be in circulation because it offers rare insights into the intersection of political and literary life under Tito, especially as refracted through the person of Kiš, who prided himself on is ability to stay out of petty Party-related squabbling.

The prose poems in this volume are as varied in subject as they are in rhythm and color. Many seem to have a lot in common with certain of Kiš's fiction. For instance, "Lighthouse Excursion" is reminiscent of the maritime melancholy of the story "The End of the Summer," and "Poem about a Poem" invokes the same detached attention to inquiry, making a theme out of method itself, as "Shoes." And there is exquisite overlap between "Tropical Nights" and certain "trippy" chapters in the novel *The Attic*, as well as in the poem "Sunset," which is arguably (in the translator's opinion) the finest poem in this volume. "The Lights of the Big City," on the other hand, is a pure surrealistic delight, and "Novo Groblje," working in a similar vein, is too complex and unique to be easily labeled.

Conclusion

These poems offer, of course, many insights into, or echoes of, aspects of Kiš's fiction beyond the autobiographical: the omnipresence and multifariousness of death; the lapidary descriptions of the two piano pieces and the two still lifes, ratcheted up to another level of painterly potency in "Sunset" and "Apollinaire Dreams of Life"; the filial longing of "Farewell, Mother"; and the postmodern clawing together of and pawing around amidst anthropological assemblages, in the form of lists of *realia*, in "Anatomy of a Scent" and, especially, "Garbage Dump." And of course there are the differences: the pronounced surrealism of many of the pieces, the juvenilia (oh, the optimism of "Tomorrow"!), and the poetic oddity of the stormy, garrulous "Golden Rain" which, while not incompatible with certain of Kiš's interviews on his practices of writing, offers up dense and painful suggestions of works unwritten and demographic dead-ends (as Kiš more or less referred to his own family tree).

These are poems of loyalty and love and loss, keenly observed; of death and eroticism; of family tragedy; and of a fascination with the enumeration of things in an indifferent or lethal world. There is an omnipresent sense of danger, a looming shadow of multifarious peril, above all of the Shoah, haunting the careful, prismatic descriptions.

John K. Cox
Fargo, North Dakota, 2018

For Further Reading

For those wishing to explore the Serbian originals, the source for these translations is the following volume:

Danilo Kiš, *Pesme, Elektra*, edited by Mirjana Miočinović, Beograd: BIGZ, 1995. This well-edited volume contains extensive notes on the origins and publication history of the poems. The dates given at the end of the English translations at hand originate from these notes and refer to the most likely dates of composition of the respective poems, some of which were only published posthumously.

For those interested in Danilo Kiš and the context in which he lived, I recommend, *Mark Thompson's Birth Certificate: The Story of Danilo Kiš* (Ithaca, NY: Cornell University Press, 2013).

Finally, a number of translations of the works of Danilo Kiš are available in English:

An American Story: Uncollected Fiction. Translated by John K. Cox. Szeged: AMERICANA eBooks, 2016.

The Attic: A Novel. Translated and with an introduction by John K. Cox. Champaign, IL: Dalkey Archive Press, 2012.

Early Sorrows (For Children and Sensitive Readers). Translated by Michael Henry Heim. New York: New Directions, 1998.

The Encyclopedia of the Dead. Translated by Michael Henry Heim. New York: Farrar, Straus and Giroux, 1989.

Garden, Ashes: A Novel. Translated by William J. Hannaher. San Diego: Harcourt Brace and Company, 1975.

Homo Poeticus: Essays and Interviews. Edited and with an introduction by Susan Sontag. New York: Farrar, Straus and Giroux, 1995.

Hourglass: A Novel. Translated by Ralph Manheim. New York: Farrar, Straus Giroux, 1990.

The Lute and the Scars: Stories. Translated and with an afterword by John K. Cox. Champaign, IL: Dalkey Archive Press, 2012.

Night and Fog: The Collected Dramas and Screenplays. Translated by John K. Cox. St. Helena, CA: Helena History Press, 2014.

"The Paris Trip," translated by John K. Cox, in *Hourglass Literary Magazine*, No. 1 (January 2017), 137-151.

Psalm 44: A Novel. Translated and with an afterword by John K. Cox. Champaign, IL: Dalkey Archive Press, 2012.

A Tomb for Boris Davidovich. Translated by Duška Mikić-Mitchell. New York: Harcourt Brace Jovanovich, 1978.